CH

MEXICAN TEXTILE TECHNIQUES

SHIRE ETHNOGRAPHY

2

Cover photograph
Trique Indians in San Andrés Chicahuaxtla, Oaxaca. The weaver uses a
backstrap loom. She and her female companions wear everyday clothing,
consisting of a wrap-around skirt, a sash and a long weft-brocaded *huipil* (tunic)
of wool, acrylic and cotton.
(Photograph: Chloë Sayer.)

In memory of Raúl Kamffer

British Library Cataloguing in Publication Data:
Sayer, Chloë
Mexican textile techniques. — (Shire ethnography; 9).
1. Mexican textiles.
I. Title.
746'. 0972.
ISBN 0-85263-970-8.

Published by
SHIRE PUBLICATIONS LTD
Cromwell House, Church Street, Princes Risborough,
Aylesbury, Bucks HP17 9AJ, UK.

Series Editor: Bryan Cranstone.

ISBN 0 85263 970 8

First published 1988

Set in 11 point Times and printed in Great Britain by
C. I. Thomas & Sons (Haverfordwest) Ltd,
Press Buildings, Merlins Bridge, Haverfordwest, Dyfed.

Contents

Acknowledgements

I wish to acknowledge the contribution of Bodil Christensen, Donald and Dorothy Cordry, Irmgard Weitlaner Johnson, Elsie McDougall, Walter F. Morris and Carlota Mapelli Mozzi and to thank Elizabeth Carmichael and Ruth D. Lechuga for their encouragement and advice over many years. Permission to publish photographs of their collections was kindly granted by the Museo Nacional de Antropología in Mexico, and by the Museum of Mankind and the Victoria and Albert Museum in England. In addition the Pitt Rivers Museum has allowed me to reproduce a photograph from their archive. I am also indebted to David Lavender, Ava Vargas and the late Marcos Ortiz for the use of their photographs. The Royal Botanic Gardens at Kew have answered several queries. My thanks are due to Bryan Cranstone for his help in producing this book. Fieldwork was carried out in Chiapas with a grant from the Winston Churchill Memorial Trust, and in the Sierra de Puebla while making a textile collection for the Museum of Mankind. I am grateful to the many spinners, dyers and weavers in Mexico who have explained and demonstrated their techniques with such patience, skill and generosity. Where not otherwise stated, the illustrations and photographs are the author's copyright.

4

List of illustrations

1
Introduction

Mexican textiles have a vigour that is unsurpassed elsewhere in the Americas. More than four and a half centuries have elapsed since the Spanish Conquest, yet nearly sixty different Indian peoples still live in Mexico. Many wear highly distinctive costumes and retain complex spinning, dyeing and weaving methods inherited from their ancestors. The Spanish legacy should not be overlooked, however. After the Conquest European materials and textile techniques were adopted in Mexico, together with a wide range of garments. Contemporary Mexican costume owes its richness and variety to this fusion of clothing styles and textile skills from the Old and New Worlds.

Geography

Few countries have such extreme variations of landscape, vegetation and climate as Mexico. Fertile valleys, tropical lowland forests, arid deserts, high mountain peaks and deep canyons together cover over 761,600 square miles (1,972,500 square km), making Mexico the third largest country in Latin America. Shaped like a great funnel or cornucopia, Mexico shares her northern border with the United States of America, and her south-eastern border with Guatemala and Belize. To the west is the Pacific Ocean, to the east lie the Gulf of Mexico and the Caribbean Sea. The central landmass is an uneven plateau flanked by the mountain ranges of the Sierra Madre, which run roughly parallel to both coastlines and rise to heights of over 2 miles (3000 metres). Contrasting environmental conditions and a wide range of raw materials have influenced the evolution of costume throughout Mexico's long history and have fostered the variety of clothing styles in use today.

Mexico before the Conquest

Most archaeologists believe that man first entered the New World from Asia across the Bering Strait during the last ice age, more than 40,000 years ago. Small nomadic bands of hunters moved southwards, gradually fanning out across North, Central and South America. Over long periods of time separate cultures developed, without any proven outside influence until the arrival of the Spaniards many centuries later.

In Mexico rudimentary forms of agriculture were evident by

1. Chinantec woman's predominantly red and white everyday cotton *huipil* from San Lucas Ojitlán, Oaxaca. Plain- and gauze-woven in three webs on a backstrap loom, it features trimmings of crocheted lace and ribbon, and embroidered designs done in running stitch. These include double-headed birds and suggest pre-Conquest styles of decoration. 31 by 35½ inches (78.7 by 90.2 cm). (Museum of Mankind. Copyright: David Lavender.)

5000 BC and archaeological examples of basketry, twining and net-ting have been dated to approximately the same period. Soon after 2500 BC the first pottery of central Mexico appeared, followed by loom weaving and by the establishment of permanent settlements. Not all village cultures progressed at the same rate, however. The first distinctive civilisation to emerge in Mexico was that of the Olmec, who inhabited the tropical lowlands of the Gulf coast and built large ceremonial centres between *c*. 1000 and 400 BC.

During the Classic era (AD 300 to 900) a cultural florescence throughout Mexico brought great advances in architecture and the other arts (figure 3). The Post-Classic age (AD 900 to 1519) saw the appearance of metallurgy and a new emphasis on militarism. Peoples of this period worshipped fierce warlike gods and with these cults came the spread of human sacrifice. In central Mexico a vast empire was created by the Toltec, who remained a dominant power during the tenth and eleventh centuries.

Meanwhile in the south and south-east other cultures had risen to prominence. The Maya excelled as architects, muralists, sculptors and potters (figure 4); they also devised complex calen-dar systems and recorded their calculations with hieroglyphic inscriptions. Maya civilisation seems to have been based on a loose federation of city states; their territories covered over 117,000 square miles (303,000 square km) and included the Yucatán Penin-sula, Tabasco and Chiapas in Mexico, together with Belize, Guatemala and parts of Honduras and El Salvador. To the west of the Maya zone highly distinctive cultures were also forged by the Zapotec and the Mixtec.

The last great pre-Conquest civilisation to evolve in Mexico was that of the Aztec. They settled in the Valley of Mexico in the mid thirteenth century and eventually built up an empire that stretched from the Gulf coast to the Pacific, reaching northwards as far as the desert and southwards into the mountains of Oaxaca. When Her-nán Cortés and his fellow Spaniards reached Mexico in 1519, they marvelled at the splendour of the Aztec capital, the magnificent clothing of the emperor and his nobles, and the artistry of dyers and weavers. In a report to the King of Spain, Cortés wrote: 'Moc-tezuma gave me a large quantity of his own textiles which, consid-ering they were cotton and not silk, were such that there could not be fashioned or woven anything similar in the whole world for the variety and naturalness of the colours and for the handiwork.'

Spanish records offer valuable information about pre-Conquest textile techniques among the Aztec and other peoples such as the Maya. Weavers worked not just with white cotton but with a brown

2. Map of Mexico.
1. Norogachic (Tarahumara). 2. Saltillo. 3.
San Andrés Cohamiata (Huichol). 4. Tux-
pan (Nahua). 5. Santa María del Río. 6.
Mezquital Valley (Otomí). 7. Tenango de
Doria (Otomí). 8. Santa Ana Hueytlalpan
(Otomí). 9. Atla; Xolotla (Nahua). 10. San
Pablito (Otomí). 11. Cuetzalan, San
Andrés Tzicuilan (Nahua). 12. San Juan
Ixtenco (Otomí). 13. Hueyapan (Nahua).
14. Tejupilco. 15. Santiago Temoaya
(Otomí). 16. Cuanajo (Tarascan). 17. Acat-
lán (Nahua). 18. San Miguel Metlatonoc
(Mixtec). 19. Xochistlahuaca (Amuzgo).
20. Pinotepa de Don Luis; Pinotepa
Nacional (Mixtec). 21. Jamiltepec (Mix-
tec). 22. Santa María Zacatepec (Tacuate).
23. Ixtayutla (Tacuate). 24. San Andrés
Chicahuaxtla (Trique). 25. San Mateo
Peñasco (Mixtec). 26. San Sebastián
Peñoles (Mixtec). 27. San Lucas Ojitlán
(Chinantec). 28. Teotitlán del Valle
(Zapotec). 29. Yalalag (Zapotec). 30.
Santo Tomás Jalieza (Zapotec). 31. Santo
Tomás Mazaltepec (Zapotec). 32. Tehuan-
tepec (Zapotec). 33. San Mateo del Mar
(Huave). 34. Venustiano Carranza (Tzot-
zil). 35. San Juan Chamula; Zinancantán
(Tzotzil). 36. San Andrés Larrainzar (Tzot-
zil). 37. Magdalenas (Tzotzil). 38. Najá
(Lacandón).

3. (Left) Pottery figurine of the Classic period from Teotihuacán in the Valley of Mexico. Garments shown include a wrap-around skirt and a *quechquemitl*. (Copyright: Museo Nacional de Antropología.)

4. (Right) Pottery figurine of the Late Classic period from Jaina, showing a Maya woman wearing a wrap-around skirt under a lozenge-patterned *huipil*. (Copyright: Museo Nacional de Antropología.)

strain still in use today. For warmth, cotton could be interspun with downy feathers or fur from the soft underbelly of rabbits and hares. Spanish observers also noted that smooth and flexible cloth was woven from agave and similar fibres. The colours praised by Cortés were obtained with a range of dyestuffs. Indigo and logwood were among the many vegetable colourants used, and from the animal world cochineal and shellfish dye were much prized.

Textiles were intricately patterned on the backstrap loom. Alternatively, finished cloth could be decorated with embroidery, freehand painting or onlay work using feathers, shells and other ornaments. Garments may also have been printed with pottery stamps or, as some illustrations suggest, patterned through tie dyeing. A fragment of pre-Conquest cloth from the Maya area proves in addition that batik methods were understood. Men in ancient Mexico wore a range of garments. These included loincloths, hipcloths, kilts, sashes, tunics, woven or netted capes, sandals and often spectacular head-dresses. Women wore wrap-around skirts and waist-sashes. Some, according to region, wore a closed shoulder-cape called a *quechquemitl* or a tunic called a *huipil*. These female garments and some male garments are still in use today.

Mexico after the Conquest

By 1521 Spanish victory over the Aztec and their allies had been secured. The contradictions underlying the Conquest were many. Spain had recently put an end to almost eight hundred years of Moorish occupation and had lost a hitherto constant supply of war booty. Mexico was to prove an alternative source of wealth, but the hunger for gold was matched by a desire to win converts for the Catholic church. Temples and idols were razed to the ground and replaced by churches and cathedrals, much of the country was divided into huge estates, and Indians in accessible areas were reduced to the level of slaves.

Although the cultivation of cotton continued unabated under Spanish rule, silk plantations were established and wool flocks introduced. To accompany these new materials, settlers also imported various features of European technology. These included the spinning wheel and wool cards for the preparation of wool, winding frames for spun yarn, scissors and needles of steel, and the treadle loom. Weaving had traditionally been a female task in Mexico, but working patterns slowly underwent a change as men were taught to operate the new looms which were faster than backstrap looms and capable of producing broader cloth. Women also acquired new skills, often in mission centres. Spanish needlework at the time of the Conquest included a wide variety of stitches, many of which are thought to have originated in ancient Egypt, Persia and other parts of the Near East. The majority of

5. (Left) Mixtec woman spinning thread with a spindle. Methods are unchanged today. (Codex Vindobonensis.)

6. (Right) Serpent and bird design from a flat clay stamp excavated near Toluca, Mexico State.

7. Few pre-Hispanic textiles have survived in Mexico because of adverse climatic conditions. These narrow strips of cloth from Coahuila have been dated to between AD 1000 and 1600. (Top) Yucca fibre, dyed and undyed, plain-woven on a loom with end-to-end warp locking. Length: 48 inches (122 cm). (Bottom) Agave fibre, dyed and undyed, knotless netting. Length: 50¾ inches (129 cm). (Copyright: Museo Nacional de Antropología.)

8. Nineteenth-century cotton panel of drawn threadwork. Selected threads have been pulled out; the rest have been bound to form a square-meshed ground and reinforced with decorative stitching. Mexico's national emblem is surrounded by small birds. 13½ inches (34.3 cm) square. (Victoria and Albert Museum, T.285-1928. Copyright: David Lavender.)

9. Nineteenth-century two-web Saltillo *sarape*, tapestry-woven on a treadle loom with a cotton warp. Natural dyes have been used for the wool weft. 62 by 94 inches (157.5 by 238.7 cm). (Museum of Mankind. Copyright: David Lavender.)

these were adopted in Mexico, which already had its own history of native embroidery, and further inspiration was provided by imported textiles from China and the Philippines. Other Old World textile techniques included drawn threadwork (figure 8), lace-making, pleating and appliqué.

Throughout the colonial period the ruling class dressed with great splendour, whilst following the fashions of Europe. The abolition of the old social hierarchy and the imposition of Christianity had far-reaching effects on native dress. Spanish friars were shocked by nudity and men came under pressure to adopt shirts and to abandon the loincloth in favour of trousers. Female costume sustained fewer changes, although women who went bare-breasted were encouraged to wear blouses.

Spanish rule came to an end in 1821. Periods of turmoil and economic crisis alternated over the next ninety years with stretches of political stability. Although the rich continued to dress in a European manner, two essentially Mexican garments found wide popularity with all social classes. One was the *sarape,* or rectangular blanket, which represented the perfect match of two foreign elements — the treadle loom and sheep's wool (figure 9). Tapestry-woven with weft threads of many colours, *sarapes* often displayed complex geometric markings and some also incorporated silk or gold and silver metallic threads. Wealthy men could afford veritable works of art. Several weaving centres achieved fame during the eighteenth and nineteenth centuries, but *sarapes* from the town of Saltillo in the northern state of Coahuila were considered superior to all others. An equivalent female garment was the *rebozo,* or rectangular shawl. Generally woven on backstrap looms, *rebozos* were worn in town and country. Expensive examples were richly embroidered, or woven from ikat-dyed thread and patterned with delicate reptilian markings. Shawls of the second type were chiefly produced in Santa María del Río in the state of San Luis Potosí.

The nineteenth century also saw the rise of the national textile industry. Freed from Spanish trade restrictions, it entered a period of expansion. Huge plantations were created in northern Mexico to provide cotton in vast quantities, synthetic dyes were imported from Europe and new technology was introduced into the factories. Cloth sales increased rapidly, yet traditionally woven cloth was still required for the garments just described and for native costumes in Indian villages.

In 1910 a new attempt was made to redress the social balance and to bridge the chasm between rich and poor. After the Revolution,

10. Otomí family from San Pablito, Puebla. The man wears a gala shirt sewn with glass beads. The women wear wrap-around skirts and wide woollen waist-sashes. Their *quechquemitl* incorporate curved woollen bands shaped on the backstrap loom and show two styles of decoration done in cross-stitch.

which lasted several years, much was done to redistribute the land. Intermarriage over the centuries between Spaniards and Indians had created a vast *mestizo* class which now outnumbered all other racial groups. As a great wave of nationalism swept the country, the people of Mexico found a new pride in their Indian past, traditions and folk arts, which had for so long been viewed as inferior to European culture.

Modern Mexico

In the late twentieth century there has been a massive expansion in Mexico's population, which exceeded 77 million in 1986. Mexico

City, built where the ancient Aztec capital once stood, is one of the largest and most modern cities in the world: in 1987 its population was approximately 17 million. Clothing here and in the other towns differs little from that worn in Europe or the United States. Despite the lure of urban life, however, over half the Mexican population still lives in rural areas and works the land. Highways and networks of roads are being built each year to connect different parts of the country, but the ruggedness of the landscape remains a major obstacle to modernisation.

Mexico's widely varying geography has contributed greatly to the sense of independence felt by many Indian peoples. Although it is hard to obtain reliable census figures in harsh and isolated regions, the Indian population is currently estimated at around 15 per cent of the national total. In remote parts of Mexico many Indian groups still lead a surprisingly marginal existence. Others, in more accessible areas, have joined the national culture while retaining a number of their own traditions. Since the Conquest many Indian languages have disappeared, but nearly sixty remain. Mutually unintelligible, these often comprise numerous local dialects. Speakers of Náhuatl, the ancient Aztec language, exceed one million, whereas some Indian languages are spoken by just a few hundred people.

Settlement patterns vary. Some Indians prefer to live in closely knit villages, while other communities are made up of family units scattered in small settlements over vast distances. Natural surroundings provide basic building materials and most families depend for their survival upon agriculture. The staple diet, as in ancient times, is composed of beans, squash, chilli peppers and maize. Although a few Indian peoples continue to worship a pantheon of gods, whom they identify with the forces of nature, most are nominal Catholics with beliefs and ceremonies which frequently hark back to the traditions of their ancestors. Continuity with the past is further reflected by crafts such as pottery and basketry, and by the textile arts. Many Indian groups have adhered to a particular style of dress, with variations to distinguish different villages. Costume acts as a bond which unites people from the same community by proclaiming their cultural and geographical origins.

2
Materials

Fibres

Mexico's varied geography and climate foster a wide range of trees, shrubs and plants, many of which provide strong and flexible fibres for weaving. These fall into three categories. The first comprises leaf fibres from monocotyledonous plants. Generally termed 'hard', these fibres are for the most part long, white and smooth. Before the Conquest yarns were often derived in northern zones from certain species of yucca, but this practice died out long ago.

The Mexican agave, by contrast, is still a source for fibres in many parts of the country. This hardy genus, which includes some two hundred species, flourishes in semi-desert regions. *Agave zapupe*, for example, is used by the Huastec Indians of Veracruz, who strip the leaves of pulp by pulling them between two sticks; the fibres are then left to dry and are occasionally dyed before being woven into durable shoulder-bags. The Otomí in the arid and inhospitable Mezquital Valley of Hidalgo rely on local agave plants to provide them with house-building materials, natural fencing, food, sweet sap which they drink, soap pulp, nails, needles, pins and textile yarns. Men are generally responsible for stripping the fibres, as the task requires great strength. The spikes are severed, baked until soft, left in water to rot, beaten with a mallet and spread across an inclined board to be scraped with a metal blade. When the fibres are free of pulp, they are soaked in water with soap, maize dough or local seeds, dried in the sun and combed.

Bast fibres, from the inner bark of dicotyledonous plants, make up the second category. In pre-Hispanic times Indian peoples made use of two or more such plants. One of these — *Urtica caracasana,* popularly known as *chichicastle* — is still used in a small area of Oaxaca where the upper branches of shrubs are boiled in water with oak ashes to act as a bleaching and softening agent. The resulting thread, when spun, is not unlike linen.

Cotton seed-pod fibres, the third category, provide the most widely used of all textile yarns. It is generally agreed that *Gossypium hirsutum* is indigenous to the New World, together with the toffee-brown strain referred to by botanists as *Gossypium mexicanum* and popularly known as *coyuche.* Among Indians cotton growing has remained a marginal pursuit, quite divorced from the high production levels of industry, which in any case has shown no interest in cultivating *coyuche*. Preparation methods for both types of cotton are long and laborious. Spinners carefully separate the fibres from the seed by hand and remove all impurities. The cotton is then fluffed out, spread on a thick blanket or palm mat and beaten with two wooden sticks (figure 11). Eventually it is shaped into a smooth, even strip and rolled up in a ball ready to be spun.

All the materials mentioned above are native to Mexico. Since its introduction in the sixteenth century, however, wool has gained wide acceptance. Today it is second only to cotton in the field of Indian costume and is especially popular in cold and mountainous regions. In many communities women are responsible for the grazing and shearing of sheep. Wool is washed, sometimes with a special soap made from local plants, and generally carded with a pair of crude boards inset with wire bristles. Weavers in many villages rely on black, brown, grey and white wool to pattern cloth. In the state of Morelos, however, Nahua women from Hueyapan have an unusual method for obtaining shades which are not naturally available: giant teasels, regularly used instead of wool cards, rub differently coloured fibres together and in this way white is mixed with brown or black to give beige or grey.

Silk is rare and greatly valued in Indian Mexico. Its cultivation by Spanish settlers, although initially successful, was later banned by royal decree when Spain's own silk industry became fearful of competition. Small-scale production continued in remote areas but was again threatened in the 1930s when widespread spraying against malaria killed off large numbers of silkworm. Fortunately, enough insects and mulberry trees persist in the mountains of Oaxaca to provide Mixtec weavers in San Sebastián Peñoles with a regular, if small, supply of silk. When boiled in water with ashes, cocoons turn from yellow to white. Once dry, they can be pulled apart and spun. Silk thread is used locally but also traded across long distances.

When the Spaniards introduced the domesticated Asiatic silkworm, *Bombyx mori*, into Mexico, they believed they were introducing silk itself. Other types of moth also yield silk filaments, however, and native species may have been in use before the Conquest but not identified by foreign observers. Today wild silk is woven in a few highland communities in Oaxaca and Puebla.

Spinning
Although most yarns are spun, there are rare exceptions: for example, silk in San Mateo Peñasco in Oaxaca is hand-twisted.

Before the Conquest netted and woven textiles in the north were frequently made from hand-twisted yucca or agave yarn and today the custom persists in mountain villages in Chiapas where Tzotzil men roll agave fibres on their legs with the palms of their hands.

11. Nahua woman beating brown cotton outside Cuetzalan, Puebla. When the fibres begin to adhere together, the blows become stronger. The cotton is turned to ensure regular beating.

The resulting twine is used to make hard-wearing shoulder-bags which are netted with the aid of a small wooden frame.

In treadle-loom workshops, where wool is needed in large quantities, the European spinning wheel is commonly used. In most Indian villages, however, spinning is still done in pre-Conquest fashion with the aid of a spindle. Whorls and their wooden shafts vary considerably in size and shape. The Tarahumara of

12. Nahua woman spinning cotton with a spindle in San Andrés Tzicuilan, Puebla.

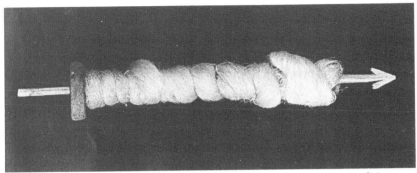

13. Otomí spindle for use with agave fibre from the Mezquital Valley, Hidalgo.(Museum of Mankind. Copyright: David Lavender.)

Chihuahua weave only wool: this is carded by hand, twisted into strands by being rolled upon the thigh, and spun into coarse thread with a wooden whorl measuring 6 inches (15.3 cm) across and a stick up to 14 inches (35.6 cm) long. Often spindles are weighted with clay whorls. These may be ancient, archaeological examples found on neighbouring land or they may be newly made either by individual families or in specialist production centres. The largely Mixtec town of Jamiltepec in Oaxaca, for example, is known for its decoratively painted clay whorls which are used throughout the region to spin cotton, silk and even wool. Spinners often show great resourcefulness: the Huichol, who live high up in the north-western Sierra Madre, have been known to make whorls from sections of gourd, bone and even broken china.

Yarn is spun by whirling the stick-and-whorl with the right hand in a dish or half-gourd, or on smooth ground, while the left hand feeds the fibres on to the tip of the spindle-shaft (figure 12). Most women kneel on a palm mat as they spin, although some prefer to sit on a low chair. However, the Otomí of the Mezquital Valley have a unique way of working. Their spindles, which are arrow-shaped at the top end, are designed for agave fibres and spin not on the ground but in the air (figure 13). Women position great hanks of unspun fibre over their right shoulders and spin while walking to market or tending their sheep and goats.

Hand-spun yarns in Mexico range from the very coarse to the very fine and the spinning time taken varies accordingly. It might take a spinner three days to turn 2 pounds (0.9 kg) of wool into thick thread, but up to two weeks to spin the same amount finely. Ultimately the texture and durability of cloth will depend upon the smoothness and resistance of the thread from which it is woven.

Dyes and dyeing methods

Yarns which are hand-spun are often dyed. Since their introduction, synthetic dyes have largely overtaken natural colouring methods. Most are aniline and work on traditional fibres, including agave, but in some weaving centres there has been a shift back to natural dyes. This has been the case in the *sarape*-producing town of Teotitlán del Valle, where Zapotec treadle-loom weavers work largely for the tourist market. In the early 1970s tapestry-woven blankets were usually brilliantly coloured, but the marked preference shown by purchasers for muted colours has prompted several weavers to rediscover natural dyeing methods. (Others, it should be said, merely claim to have done so. Despite appearances, the fashionable pastel shades of some *sarapes* in Teotitlán del Valle are still the result of synthetic colourants.)

Some weavers have never abandoned natural dyes and a surprisingly wide range are still in use throughout Mexico. Traditional techniques require considerable skill, hard work and patience: operations can take several hours or several days. Ingredients are rarely measured, as weavers work mostly by guesswork. As in the past, dyes are obtained from vegetable, animal and mineral sources. Some are substantive and stain fibres directly; others require mordants to fix them.

Leaves, fruits, flowers, barks and woods all provide regional dyes, but the plant species most widely used today is indigo, *Indigofera anil*. During the early years of Conquest its rich blue-black tones were much appreciated in Europe and sizable fortunes were made by those who exploited it. Today indigo is grown for home consumption only and often traded across long distances. To break down the indigo, dyers soak it for several days in water, or sometimes in lye, a liquid made from lime, wood and the charcoal ashes of pine and oak. When a dough-like consistency is reached, the indigo is beaten to paste and returned to the vat with water. Yarns are dipped in this solution two or three times daily for up to five days. After each soaking they are wrung out and hung up to dry so that oxidisation can take place and with each immersion the colour deepens.

Other more localised plant dyes offer a wide spectrum of colours. In the highlands of Chiapas, grey with purplish-blue overtones is obtained with *muicle, Jacobinia spicigera*, when it is mordanted with lime, alum and chrome. Various shades of tan and red are achieved with brazilwood, *Haematoxylum brasiletto*, and logwood, *Haematoxylum campechianum*. Lichens mixed with alum provide the Tarahumara with rusty yellow, while in the Chiapas

14. Mixtec wrap-around skirt, woven in three webs on a backstrap loom, from Pinotepa de Don Luis, Oaxaca. The horizontally worn stripes incorporate cochineal-dyed silk, dark-blue cotton dyed with indigo, and lilac cotton dyed with the secretion of shellfish. 60½ by 45½ inches (153.7 by 115.6 cm). (Copyright: Museum of Mankind.)

15. (Below) Ikat-patterned Otomí *quechquemitl,* photographed in the 1930s by Elsie McDougall. This style was apparently current among the Otomí of Querétaro, Hidalgo and Toluca. (Copyright: Pitt Rivers Museum.)

highlands lichens dye a reddish brown and dogwood leaves are used with alum or chrome to give varying shades of yellow. Other colourants include the seeds of *annatto, Bixa orellana*, which stain a rusty orange, blackberries, which are a source of purple, camomile leaves, which give a greenish gold, and countless other plants which meet local needs and go by local names but remain unidentified by botanists.

Inorganic substances, usually found in natural deposits, play a vital role in many dyeing processes. Lime, alum and chrome have already been mentioned. Iron oxide, gypsum and ochres furnish stable pigments when mixed with other elements. Ruth D. Lechuga has observed an interesting procedure in Santa María del Río and Tejupilco, in the states of San Luis Potosí and Mexico: old iron, left to decompose in water, provides the basis for a black and strong-smelling dye. This is used for *rebozos,* which retain a permanent odour and are therefore termed *de olor.*

Two animal dyes, greatly valued before and after the Conquest, persist today, despite growing rarity and high prices. *Purpura patula pansa* is a species of shellfish, or sea-snail, which is currently exploited only along isolated coastal stretches of southern Oaxaca. In winter Mixtec men from the inland village of Pinotepa de Don Luis carry a quantity of spun cotton thread to the Pacific shore. At low tide the dyers pick the molluscs off the wet rocks in order to squeeze and blow on them, and the foamy secretion which they then give off is rubbed on to the yarn. The liquid is colourless at first, but contact with the air makes it turn yellow, green and, ultimately, purple. Molluscs are returned unharmed to the rocks, left for up to a month while the dyers work their way along the coast, and then 'milked' a second time. After repeated washings shellfish-dyed yarn softens to a delicate lavender, but according to popular belief it never loses the tang of the sea.

When Mexico was a Spanish colony, shipments of cochineal to Europe ranked second only to precious metals. Subsequently the industry was allowed to decline, but production continues on a small scale. Domesticated cochineal, *Dactylopius coccus,* is a delicate insect which feeds on host cacti belonging to the *Opuntia* or *Nopalea* genus. Pregnant females are settled, or 'seeded', on the joints of the plants. After approximately one hundred days the new parasites are harvested and enough females retained for a new cycle. Indians also collect wild cochineal from untended cacti, but the dye yield is not as good.

The eventual colour of cochineal-dyed yarn is determined by a number of factors. The insects may be sun-dried or toasted on griddles, before being ground to powder and mordanted with alum, lime juice or salt. Wool and silk are both extremely receptive and dyers can achieve not just red and pink, but also near-black and even purple shades. According to Amber Spark, who has made a study of dyeing methods in the Chiapas highlands, weavers in the region first mordant wool with alum and then boil the wool in a mixture of ground cochineal, water and lime juice. Dyed in this way, yarns do not fade but turn darker with age.

Until recently many of these natural dyes were used in conjunction with ikat. This technique takes its name from the Indonesian word *mengikat,* which means 'to tie'. Ikat-dyed yarns are patterned before they are woven: stretched between two sticks, they are tightly bound at predetermined intervals with thread. When the skein is dipped in the dye bath, the covered portions are 'reserved'. If this procedure is to be repeated, the weaver binds new sections and dips the skein in dye of a different colour. It is usual to begin with lighter shades and progress to darker ones. In Mexico it is the warp yarns which are ikat-dyed. Rarely figurative, designs are characterised by the blurred outlines which occur when the dye begins to penetrate reserved areas.

Although archaeological remains confirm the existence of ikat techniques in northern Peru, no pre-Conquest examples have so far been found in Mexico. If not indigenous, ikat may have been introduced under Spanish rule, either from south-east Asia or from the Middle East via Italy and Mallorca. Today it remains the most widely admired form of decoration for *rebozos,* which are woven in a number of centres and worn by Indian and *mestizo* women alike. Delicately dappled *rebozos* of silk from Santa María del Río fetch large sums of money; cotton or rayon examples are more modestly priced.

Synthetic fibres

Since the 1960s there has been a worldwide trend towards synthetic fibres and Mexico is no exception. Many weavers now prefer, or are compelled by shortages, to buy silk substitutes and to replace wool with acrylic. Factory yarns save labour and come in a dazzling range of colours which have affected local tastes in several areas. The Huichol have enthusiastically adopted acrylic yarns in luminescent shades of lime green, acid yellow and shocking pink, matching them in startling combinations. For fine work, these may be re-spun in traditional fashion.

Although new materials and colours undoubtedly have inspirational value, their adoption can also bring negative consequences. When a weaver accustomed to gathering and preparing her own materials starts to buy them, she enters the national economy and becomes vulnerable to inflation. At the same time, factory-produced fibres, whether synthetic or natural, are rarely as long-lasting as home-spun yarns, and cheap factory threads and factory dyes may not be colour-fast. The varying textures of traditionally spun yarns and the subtlety of natural dyes can rarely be matched by industry.

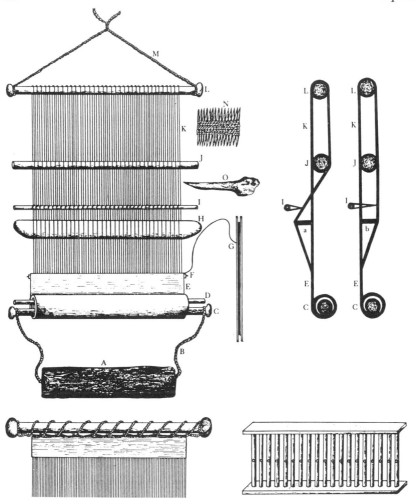

16. (Top left) Diagram of a backstrap loom. (A) backstrap; (B) cord attaching backstrap to loom; (C) front loom bar; (D) rolling stick; (E) web of woven cloth; (F) tenter attached with thorns to underside of cloth; (G) weft thread wound on to shuttle stick, or bobbin; (H) batten; (I) stick heddle attached with thread to selected warps; (J) shed stick; (K) warp threads; (L) back loom bar; (M) cord attaching loom to tree or post; (N) comb; (O) bone pick. The warp threads are wound directly round the end bars and will need to be severed when the weaving is completed. (Top right) The basic principles of weaving. The warp threads, seen in side view, form (a) the shed, and (b) the counter shed. (Bottom left) When warp threads are attached with cords to the end bars of the loom, cloth with four selvages is produced. Here the weaver has woven a heading section. (Bottom right) Rigid heddle, probably inspired by European treadle looms and used today instead of a stick heddle in some sash-weaving villages. Stiff twigs, drilled in the centre with small holes and fixed to an upper and lower bar of wood, support the warp threads. (Copyright: David Lavender.)

3
Weaving

The backstrap loom

Woven textiles are made by interlacing a series of threads, termed the 'weft', at right angles with a series of threads termed the 'warp'. Although some theories suggest that loom weaving may have been introduced into Mexico from South America, it probably evolved independently, inspired by mat-making and similar basketry methods. In central, southern and parts of northern Mexico weaving was done on the *telar de cintura,* or backstrap loom, and the custom persists today in countless Indian villages.

The apparatus is simple, with no rigid framework (figure 16), but setting it up is a lengthy process. First the weaver must organise the warp, thereby establishing the length of the textile to be made and the number of threads that form its width. If a garment is to have vertical stripes, they must be planned at this stage. The yarn is wound in a figure of eight on to a warping frame. This device often consists of upright stakes which are pushed into the ground or slotted into holes in a wooden frame; an alternative, less usual type is shown in figure 17. The threads are dipped in maize water to stiffen them and entered into the loom. If a weaver winds the warp directly round both end bars, she limits herself to cloth with side selvages. If she requires four selvages, however, the warp should be held by cords which encircle the end bars.

When the loom is in use, the bar furthest from the weaver is tied to a tree or post; the other is attached by a strap to the weaver herself, who controls the tension of the tightly stretched warps with her body. The cross, produced at the warping stage, now keeps each thread in its proper place. A shed stick is used to separate the two sets of alternate threads, which form a natural opening called a counter shed. The shuttle stick carrying the weft travels through this opening, passing over and under the same warps as the shed stick. The position of the warps is then reversed. Those warps which initially lay behind the shed stick are pulled forward to make a second opening, or shed, through which the weft travels on its return journey. A stick heddle attached by loops of thread, or, less commonly, a rigid heddle, is responsible for raising the warps in this second set; they then drop back automatically to their original position.

Loom parts, which are made by the weaver and by members of her family, also include a batten, or sword. This serves both to beat

17. Tzotzil weaver in San Juan Chamula, Chiapas, reeling yarn off a winding frame on to a warping frame in a figure of eight. The first device is of European origin, but the second is native to Mexico.

down the weft and to widen the shed and the counter shed. The weaving proceeds away from the weaver, who winds newly completed cloth on to a rolling stick. A tenter, or temple, is used to control the width of most webs; often made from a hollow reed, it is stretched across the underside of the weaving and held in place by thorns or nails. Although the loom requires a minimum of parts for plain weaving, additional tools may be used for pattern weaving. In order to subdivide warps and create further sheds, some weavers rely on a number of heddles. Short picks made from wood, bone or iron or long pointed sticks sometimes serve to lift warps and to pull up or push down wefts.

It is common practice, when starting a four-selvage web, to complete a short section at one end called a 'heading'. The loom is then reversed and the weaver begins again from the opposite end. This custom secures the spacing of the warps and prevents them from tangling. When the weaving is nearly completed, the space which remains between the heading and the main section becomes too small to receive the batten and weavers often employ a comb to push back the weft threads.

Extremely long webs of cloth can be woven on backstrap looms, but the width is limited by the weaver's armspan. If she requires a broader width than she can achieve with a single web, then two or more webs may be seamed together. During the production of lighter fabrics, women generally sit on a mat or low chair; heavy cloths can demand a kneeling or even a standing position. Dark interiors and lack of space lead most weavers to work outside the home. Because backstrap looms are so easy to roll up and transport, some weavers carry them long distances. In the countryside surrounding San Andrés Chicahuaxtla in Oaxaca, for example, brightly dressed Trique girls sometimes herd goats while they weave.

18. Tzotzil woman in San Andrés Larrainzar, Chiapas, using a backstrap loom to create plain-woven cloth with brocaded motifs; a woven central section keeps the warp threads in position. While she works, the backstrap weaver is herself part of the loom.

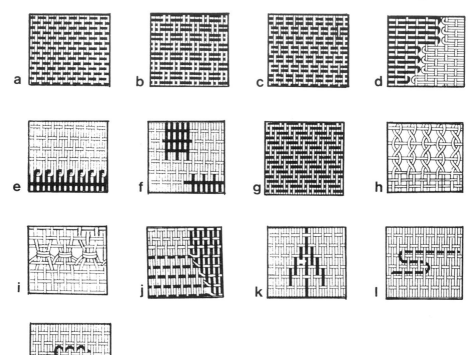

19. Weaving constructions. (The warp is drawn vertically and the weft horizontally.) (a) Plain, or tabby. Each weft thread passes over and under one warp thread. (b) Basket, or extended tabby. Warp and weft threads move in equal groups of two or more. (c) Semi-basket. One element is more numerous than the other. Here two weft threads cross one warp thread. (d) Tapestry. Cloth with one warp and a discontinuous weft composed of threads of different colours. Here weft threads are turned back around warp threads to create vertical slits. (e) End-to-end warp locking. Short warp threads, generally of different colours, are linked together. (f) Double weaving. Two sets of differently coloured warp threads are used. Each warp thread is plain-woven with a weft thread of the same colour. The two layers of cloth are periodically interchanged. (g) Twill. Diagonal lines are formed as warp threads are regularly positioned to the right or left of successive weft threads. When two warp threads pass over, then under, two weft threads, 2/2 twill is created, as here. Many variations are possible. (h) Gauze. Selected warp threads are crossed by hand. Here the technique is combined with plain weaving. (i) Weft-wrap openwork. One or more weft threads are wrapped round a group of warp threads. Generally the technique is combined with plain weaving, as here. (j) Curved weaving. *Quechquemitl* weavers are able to create shaped cloth by using a group of warp threads as weft threads. (k) Warp patterning. Warp threads cross varying numbers of weft threads to form patterns in the cloth. (l) Brocade patterning. Supplementary threads create superstructural designs. They rarely travel across the whole web. Here weft brocading is combined with plain weaving. (m) Weft-loop brocading. Supplementary weft threads are looped to form raised superstructural patterning.

Weaving constructions

As in pre-Conquest and colonial times, a wide range of patterning is achieved on the backstrap loom. Traditional garments are not cut or tailored in the European manner, but assembled directly from the squares and rectangles of cloth which the loom produces. The elegance and decorative appeal of Indian clothing derive largely, therefore, from the texture and patterning of the cloth itself. When the warp and the weft are equal in number and thickness, the cloth is described as balanced; warp- or weft-faced cloth is created when the threads of one set are dominant, because they are thicker or more numerous than those of the other set.

Plain weaving, often referred to as tabby weaving, operates on an over-one-under-one principle (figure 19,a). This basic construction is open to variation: warp and weft threads may move in equal groups of two or more (figure 19,b) or one element can outnumber the other (figure 19,c). Plain-woven cloth is often patterned with stripes by weavers of *rebozos* and wrap-around skirts. When warp threads of several colours are combined with weft threads of a single colour, warp stripes are produced. When the process is reversed, weft bands result. Checks are made by mixing warp stripes with weft bands.

Different textures can be achieved with plain weaving. In some regions extremely thick or additional weft threads are used to create raised lines in cloth. Sashes are often wholly ribbed in this way, while garments such as the *huipil* may feature groups of raised horizontal lines. Nahua weavers of *quechquemitl* in the Puebla highlands specialise in patterning cloth with occasional weft bands of *crêpe;* this is done by compressing overlong rows of weft so that they pucker.

Several other weaves are derived from tabby. In tapestry weaving the warp threads are widely spaced and covered by weft threads of different colours. These do not travel across the width of the cloth, but meet in a variety of ways; when discontinuous weft threads are looped round warp threads, tiny slits occur in the cloth (figure 19,d). This device is sometimes used by non-tapestry weavers to create vertical neck openings. In tapestry, however, the slits are stepped to avoid weakening the cloth. Alternatively, tapestry wefts may be turned round a common warp thread or linked together, thereby avoiding the creation of slits altogether. Tapestry was much practised before the Conquest and so was end-to-end warp locking (figure 19,e) but this technique is virtually unknown in modern Mexico.

Double weaving requires great skill. Today it is done only by the

20. Double-woven Otomí bags from the Mezquital Valley, Hidalgo. (Left) 12 inches (30.5 cm) square. (Right) 10½ inches (26.7 cm) square. (Copyright: David Lavender.)

Otomí of Hidalgo, the Cora of Nayarit and their closely related neighbours, the Huichol. Bags and sashes are plain-woven in two layers and two colours (figure 20). Motifs are identical on both sides of the cloth, but the colours are reversed: for example, a blue bird on a red background becomes a red bird on a blue background. This is achieved with two sets of warp threads (figure 19,f). Each set has two sheds: the first operates with two heddles, the second with a single heddle and a shed stick. Manipulations are also helped by pointed pattern sticks.

The binding system for twill weaving is different from that used in plain weaving. Each warp thread passes over two or more adjacent weft threads, then under the next one or more; or under two or more adjacent weft threads, then over the next one or more (figure 19,g). By moving the points of intersection regularly to the right or left, weavers create diagonal lines in the cloth. In Mexico twill techniques are often used to pattern woollen skirts and blankets with lozenges and zigzag motifs. According to Irmgard W. Johnson, Chocho women in Oaxaca weave two-and-two twilled blankets with three heddles, one shed stick and two pattern sticks.

Gauze weaving, used to create open-meshed cloth, has a wide distribution. It differs in concept from the loom constructions examined so far in that selected warp threads are displaced: crossed by hand, they are then secured by the weft (figure 19,h). Gauze may be combined with other weaves. In several villages in Oaxaca, for example, weavers employ gauze, plain and brocading techniques to produce fine *huipiles*. Gauze weaving is also much practised in the highlands of Puebla where Nahua weavers create *quechquemitl* with the delicacy of lace. Methods vary in this region. Women in and around Cuetzalan rely on several heddles to divide warp threads into groups. Four is the most common number, but some weavers work with twenty or more heddles to produce a range of geometric patterns. In villages such as Atla or Xolotla, however, manipulations are largely manual, even during the creation of figured gauze which includes animals, double-headed birds and other complex motifs (figure 21).

Weft-wrap openwork is another loom technique demanding

21. Detail from a Nahua *quechquemitl* of figured gauze from Xolotla, Puebla. Motifs include double-headed birds, monkeys and human figures on horseback. Approximate size of section shown: 8 by 5½ inches (20.3 by 14 cm). (Copyright: David Lavender.)

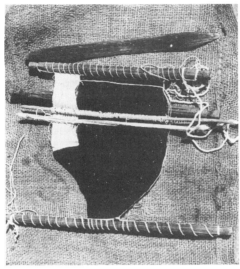

22. Unfinished *quechquemitl* web from Santa Ana Hueytlalpan, Hidalgo. In this Otomí village *quechquemitl* are unusually small. Webs are woven individually and shaped on the loom.

great skill and laborious finger manipulations. When one or more weft threads are wrapped round a group of warp threads, openings are created in the cloth (figure 19,i). Zapotec weavers in Santiago Choapan, Oaxaca, used to make all-white gala *huipiles* featuring bird, animal, flower and human motifs with a combination of weft-wrap and plain weaving methods.

The versatility of the backstrap loom is further demonstrated by curved weaving. Apparently unknown outside the Americas, this technique is practised in a small number of villages in the Puebla highlands by the Otomí, the Totonac and the Nahua. By converting a group of adjacent warp threads to weft threads, weavers are able to create cloth webs which are shaped at one corner of one end (figure 19,j). Weavers join two such webs to make gently rounded *quechquemitl*. In San Pablito both webs are woven on the same loom, whereas in Santa Ana Hueytlalpan they are woven singly (figure 22).

With warp patterning, raised designs are formed in the cloth. Warp threads, manipulated by hand, are periodically moved over and under varying numbers of weft threads (figure 19,k). Sashes are embellished in this way in a number of villages including Santo Tomás Jalieza, Oaxaca, where Zapotec weavers specialise in plant, animal and human motifs. Formerly Mixtec skirt weavers also used the technique to pattern selected warp stripes with a range of animal and plant designs.

Brocade weaves are not derived from any basic construction but

23. Warp-fringed cotton *servilleta*, or cloth, with weft brocading from the Huave village of San Mateo del Mar, Oaxaca. 29 inches (73.7 cm) square. (Copyright: David Lavender.)

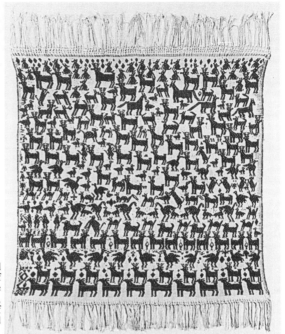

24. Woman's warp-patterned sash and pattern board of twigs and wool from the Tarascan village of Cuanajo, Michoacán. (Museum of Mankind. Copyright: David Lavender.)

25. Tarahumara women positioning the wool warp of a future blanket on a rigid loom in Norogachic, Chihuahua. (Copyright: Ava Vargas.)

have supplementary threads added to the ground weave in order to enrich the appearance of the fabric (figure 19,l). In Mexico weft brocading is the most widespread style of decoration employed by backstrap weavers (figure 23): it is used in conjunction with plain weaving for almost all categories of Indian clothing and is often mistaken for embroidery by uninitiated observers. Most garments are brocaded with brightly coloured threads, but some weavers specialise in working in white on a white background. Warp brocading is also practised in several villages for the elaboration of sashes.

Closely related to brocading is weft-loop weaving. Supplementary weft threads are pulled up with a pick to form a pattern of loops (figure 19,m). Among the lowland Totonac of Veracruz and the highland Otomí of San Pablito, Puebla, this technique is used to weave all-white *servilletas,* or cloths, of great beauty. It seems possible that this indigenous skill may have been reinforced after the Conquest by Spanish examples of weft-loop weaving, also worked entirely in white.

Most weavers carry their designs in their heads and work entirely from memory and the imagination, although cloth fragments from worn-out garments can sometimes serve as samplers for occasional consultation. Tarascan weavers in Cuanajo, Michoacán, are unusual, therefore, because they record the complex warp patterning of sashes by constructing pattern boards from twigs and wool (figure 24). The time taken to complete different types of weaving varies considerably. In the rainy season many women do not weave at all and throughout the rest of the year household tasks leave just a few hours daily for textile work. An average *huipil* takes between two and three months, but the now defunct weft-wrapped gala *huipil* from Santiago Choapan demanded around eight months.

The rigid loom

Although the backstrap loom is used throughout most of Indian Mexico, there exists a second type of native loom. Horizontal and stationary, it evolved in northern zones before the Conquest and today it is current among the Tarahumara and the Northern Tepehuan of Chihuahua and the Mayo of Sonora. Weavers from the first two Indian groups construct a rigid frame close to the ground from four crudely finished logs; two of these are notched to support the other two, which serve as raised end bars. Square or rectangular in shape, this loom lends itself to the weaving of woollen blankets and sashes. While working, women sit with their legs stretched out in front beneath the loom.

Woollen blankets are also a speciality with Mayo weavers, but their looms differ slightly because the end bars are supported by four posts set in the ground. Mayo weaving is done from a kneeling or squatting position. The principle is the same among all three groups: the warp, which is continuous, is wound round the end bars to produce tubular cloth with side selvages (figure 25). The warp is then severed, leaving the cloth with a fringe at both ends. Weavers use plain, tapestry, warp-patterning and even, on occasion, warp-brocading techniques.

The treadle loom

Weaving with native looms remains an almost exclusively female pursuit, but the Spanish treadle loom, or shaft loom, is worked by men. The warp is stretched between two end bars and crossed at right angles by the weft, as with the backstrap and rigid looms. In the case of the treadle loom, however, the end bars are incorporated into a self-contained wooden frame which permits the use of foot pedals and the automatic creation of sheds. This greatly facilitates and speeds up the weaving procedure and allows the production of long webs of cloth.

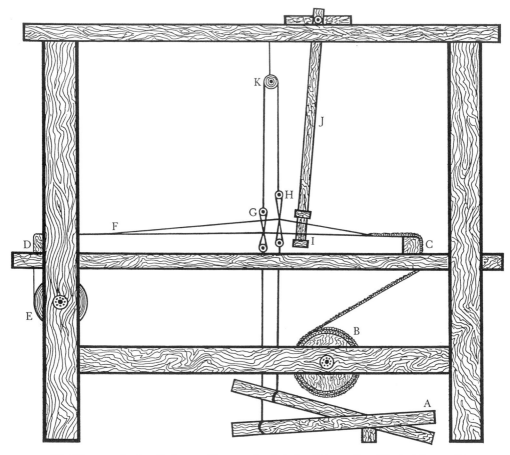

26. Diagram of a treadle loom with one pair of shafts: (A) treadles; (B) cloth beam; (C) breast beam; (D) back beam; (E) warp beam; (F) warp thread; (G) first shaft; (H) second shaft; (I) reed; (J) beater; (K) pulley. (Copyright: David Lavender.)

Most frames are built by local carpenters (figure 26). Strength and rigidity are necessary qualities, enabling looms to withstand the continual beating down of the weft. Four posts (a front pair and a back pair) are joined together by parallel side-bars; cross-bars complete this outer structure. At the back, warp yarns are wound round a warp beam and passed over a second beam. At the front, where the weaver stands, finished cloth is stretched over a breast beam and rolled on to a cloth beam. A temple serves to hold out the edges of the material being woven. This appliance reaches across the underside of the web; usually it is made from two pieces of hard wood which fit together to suit varying cloth widths. Ropes link the heddle harnesses to pedals below and to pulleys above. Each harness consists of an upper and a lower heddle bar, which are together termed a 'shaft' — hence the name 'shaft loom'. The warp is secured by leashes, or loops of thread, which run between the two bars. Wire can also be used, with eyes to accommodate the warp.

The colonial loom is counterbalanced, operating with one or two pairs of shafts. With a single pair, the shed and the counter shed are formed as follows: the first treadle is depressed and the corresponding heddle is pulled down with half the warp threads. This action creates an opening for the weft, which is carried across by the shuttle. Next the weaver operates the second treadle and brings down the second heddle with the remaining warp threads; the weft then makes its return journey through this new opening. In other words, while one half of the warp is rising the other is falling. If two pairs of shafts are used, however, the weaver has the option of raising two shafts and lowering two, or of raising one shaft while lowering three, and vice versa. Each newly inserted weft thread is beaten into position by the reed, which is fixed in a heavy swinging frame and acts like a giant comb. This device not only serves as a batten but also keeps the warp threads which pass through it evenly distributed.

Cloth production occurs in many areas of Mexico, usually in small family-run, *mestizo* workshops. Output includes skirt lengths, *rebozos* and blankets which are often bought by the local Indian population. Such textiles are generally plain-woven. They may be of a single colour, as are the indigo-blue skirt webs woven in San Cristóbal de las Casas in Chiapas, or they may feature stripes or checks.

Several varieties of twill weaving are practised in treadle-loom centres. Few contemporary examples are as fine, however, as the heavy cochineal-dyed woollen skirts with delicate lozenge patterning which were worn until the 1950s by Zapotec women in the Valley of Oaxaca. Tapestry weaving, much used for *sarapes*, is widespread in many states. The technique requires time and patience because, when designs are being formed, the weft does not travel from selvage to selvage. Yarns of different colours are wound on to bobbins and the cloth is woven in small areas.

Teotitlán del Valle in Oaxaca has long been an important centre for tapestry work and output is high. Looms, which are constructed

27. Treadle loom with two shafts from Santa Ana del Valle, Oaxaca. The male weaver is creating a tapestry-patterned *sarape* using weft yarns on cane bobbins. The photograph shows both shafts, the reed and the cloth beam which carries completed cloth. (Copyright: Marcos Ortiz.)

with a single back beam, are wider now than formerly. It was usual in the past for *sarape* weavers to join two webs together, but today there is a demand for extremely wide rugs and wall hangings. As a result looms measuring 7 feet 6 inches (2.3 metres) across and incorporating three pairs of pedals are current. Some looms even reach 13 feet 1 inch (4 metres) and require five pairs of pedals. As the weaver moves slowly from side to side, he operates the nearest pair. The temple passes across the top of the web and individual areas of pattern weft are pressed down with small wooden combs.

Market forces have influenced not just the proportions but also the designs of textiles in Teotitlán del Valle. Traditional motifs have been largely replaced by copies of European artists such as Matisse or Miró, or by Navajo patterning from North America. Not content to reproduce the designs of other countries, Isaac Vásquez Garcia has instead sought inspiration in the cultures of ancient Mexico. His workshop now produces giant tapestry-woven scenes taken from murals and codices. The cartoon, or outline of the design done on paper, hangs on the wall behind the weaver, who draws this same outline on the warp threads immediately in front of him. With so many looms working non-stop, Teotitlán del Valle requires an endless supply of sheep's wool. This is bought in from neighbouring villages and also from distant regions, but an overall shortage of wool and correspondingly high prices force many weavers here and in other *sarape* centres to use increasing amounts of acrylic yarn.

Although looms in some workshops now incorporate modern additions, the Mexican treadle loom remains in essence the direct descendant of the medieval loom which first appeared in Europe around AD 1000. However, competition from power looms is strong and, since they became established in Mexico during the nineteenth century, sales of factory-produced cloth have escalated in town and country. Today, even in remote areas, many market stalls are filled with cheap blankets, acrylic shawls and lengths of industrial cloth which threaten the future of more costly traditional textiles from native and treadle looms alike. All too often quantity overwhelms quality, but there are exceptions. In San Cristóbal de las Casas, for example, one shop-owner has introduced Jacquard-style looms. Fully mechanised, they ingeniously simulate brocade weaves. The pattern sheds are controlled by an endless chain of perforated cards; as needles penetrate each line of holes, the corresponding warp threads are raised by wires. This method of production is well suited to figured bedspreads which display repeat designs in contrasting colours.

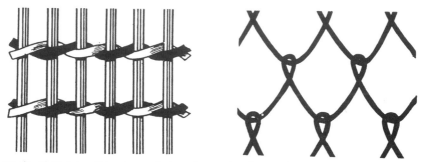

28. (Left) Twining. Here two weft threads are twisted around each other to enclose groups of warp threads. There are many variations on this procedure. (Right) Knotless netting. Successive rows of yarn are looped into the preceding row. Finished fabric may be close- or open-meshed. (Copyright: David Lavender.)

29. Some of the many embroidery stitches currently used in Mexico: (a) satin; (b) fishbone; (c) stem; (d) running; (e) chain; (f) blanket; (g) feather; (h) cross; (i) long-armed cross; (j) herringbone; (k) plain couching.

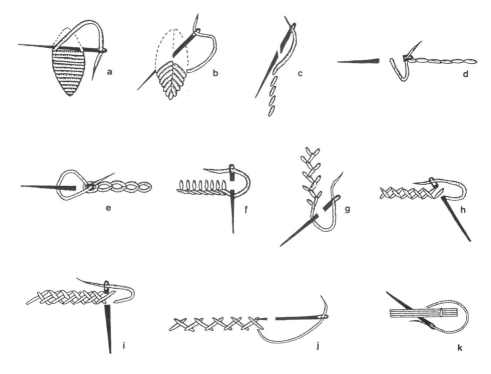

4
Additional textile techniques

Barkcloth

An ancient, though rare, survival in the costume field is bark-cloth. Archaeologists working at a number of pre-Conquest sites have found examples of cloth made from the beaten inner bark of wild fig trees of the genus *Ficus*. This was occasionally used for clothing (vestments of bark paper were worn during Aztec ceremonies) and for codices, or pictorial manuscripts. In modern Mexico bark paper is most often used for religious ceremonies and witchcraft or for the painting of decorative pictures for tourists. In the Chiapas rain forests, however, the Lacandón Indians, who belong to the Maya family, make tunics from barkcloth. First they strip long portions of bark away from the wood of the tree. When these have been immersed in water, they are spread over freshly cut trunks. Then the Lacandón beat the bark fibres with a wooden mallet until they unite and stretch, often to double their original size. Finished tunics were worn by Lacandón men during non-Christian rituals; now they are sold to collectors and museums, although red-dyed headbands of barkcloth are still offered to the Lacandón gods.

Twining and netting

These techniques, which pre-dated weaving in Mexico, are still practised in a few communities. Twining requires two elements: these are interlaced by hand, hence the alternative term 'finger weaving' (figure 28, left). Archaeological examples include sandals and clothing remains. Today no garment is wholly made by this method, but the pre-Hispanic custom of reinforcing blanket webs with twined borders persists in some villages. So too does the twining of fringes which are subsequently sewn on to the edges of *quechquemitl*.

Netting relies on the looping or knotting of a single element (figure 28, right). It was employed before the Conquest to construct articles of clothing such as capes and headbands, and cloth of great intricacy was made in Coahuila from coloured strands of agave fibre (figure 7, bottom). Today carrying bags of agave fibre are netted with the aid of a frame in several villages.

Embroidery

It is difficult, given the scarcity and the fragmentary nature of pre-Conquest textiles, to say which stitches were current before the introduction of Spanish embroidery methods. Today Mexican women decorate home-woven and bought cloth with a range of stitches using wool, cotton, silk and rayon. The availability of brightly coloured factory thread acts as an incentive to creativity and garments in some regions display increasingly large areas of needlework.

Flat stitches are extremely popular. Animals, birds, flowers and foliage are worked in satin stitch to embellish *huipiles,* skirts, blouses and *servilletas.* The gala costume worn by Zapotec women from the Isthmus of Oaxaca is particularly striking. Short *huipiles* and gathered skirts of dark velvet or sateen are satin-stitched in silk with enormous and colourful flowers; a horizontal wooden frame and a special embroidery hook are generally used. In many areas of Mexico satin stitching also serves to make decorative cloth joins in skirts and *huipiles.* Running stitch, identified in pre-Conquest cloth samples, is employed by the Mazahua to decorate skirt borders, by the Chinantec of San Lucas Ojitlán to pattern everyday *huipiles* with angular bird and snake motifs, and for Otomí and Nahua blouses in the highlands of Puebla (figure 30, top). *Pepenado fruncido*, now rare, is still a speciality in the Otomí village of San Juan Ixtenco, Tlaxcala. With this technique running stitches form areas of negative patterning on blouses, while creating tiny folds in the cloth.

Crossed stitches have had enormous impact in Mexico, and in some areas they are taking over from flat stitches. Cross and long-armed cross are used with great skill in San Pablito, Puebla, by Otomí women who embellish their *quechquemitl* and gala blouses with a range of design motifs worked in wool or acrylic (figure 30, bottom). The Huichol and the Huastec are also adept at patterning clothing in cross stitch.

Looped stitches are employed in some villages. In Pinotepa Nacional, Oaxaca, Mixtec women border the white wedding *huipil* at the neck with silk ribbon; this band is then covered with a profusion of minutely chain-stitched fish, crabs, scorpions and other creatures worked in silk floss of several colours. Blanket stitches, used before the Conquest to reinforce frayed cloth selvages, provide ornamental borders in some regions. White, gauze-woven *quechquemitl* are sometimes feather-stitched at the corners by Nahua women in Cuetzalan, Puebla.

Couching was an important skill during the colonial era, when church textiles displayed a wealth of metallic thread. With this technique, which is open to many variations, delicate threads are sewn on to the ground material with other threads. Splendid wrap-

30. Acrylic-embroidered blouses with square-cut sleeves. (Top) Designs in running stitch show the Virgin Mary with angels, lettering and plant motifs. Nahua from Coacuila, Puebla. (Bottom) Cross-stitched designs include horses, deer, squirrels and birds. Otomí from San Pablito, Puebla. (Copyright: David Lavender.)

31. Nahua woman from Santa Catarina, Puebla, wearing a *quechquemitl* of bought cotton cloth embroidered in cross stitch, with a wrap-around skirt and a warp-patterned sash.

around skirts are woven in the Nahua village of Acatlán, Guerrero, and embroidered with fanciful birds, animals, flowers and lettering, worked in synthetic silk. Stem, fishbone, satin and couching are among the methods used.

Treadle-operated sewing machines have been adopted in many Indian communities, where they seam garments and occasionally provide decorative stitching. Skirts in the states of Puebla, Veracruz and Hidalgo are sometimes enlivened with straight and undulating lines or with flower and vine motifs; blouses combine hand-embroidered motifs on the yoke with whirlpool designs in machine chain stitch across the shoulders. In Oaxaca Zapotec women on the Isthmus decorate everyday *huipiles* by criss-crossing and superimposing lines of chain stitch which have the delicacy of filigree (figure 32, top), while *huipiles* and skirts in the Maya villages of Yucatán carry a profusion of colourful satin-stitched flowers.

With a few exceptions, the art of embroidery is confined to women. It is taught, like weaving, during late childhood. Traditional designs are perpetuated by samplers, which serve as teaching aids and also as reminders in adult life. Fragments of worn-out

32. Short, close-fitting Zapotec *huipiles* from Tehuantepec, Oaxaca. (Top) Everyday *huipil* of black sateen, machine embroidered in chain stitch. 24 by 21 inches (70 by 53.3 cm). (Bottom) Gala *huipil* of velvet, embroidered in silk with large satin-stitched flowers, probably inspired by imported shawls. 21 by 18 inches (53.3 by 45.7 cm). (Copyright: David Lavender.)

garments are frequently kept as additional records of stitches and motifs. In some villages embroidery designs are drawn on to the cloth. Pattern elements are derived not just from the ancient civilisations of Mexico, but also from Europe, the Near East, China and the Philippines. However, the use of printed pattern sheets has been spreading. Design stereotypes, such as cross-stitched roses and peacocks, are becoming increasingly popular and are supplanting regional styles in a number of villages. This decline is also linked with the growing use of *cuadrillé*, or open-meshed factory cloth.

Resist-dyeing, painting and stamping

Plangi, from the Indonesian word meaning 'many-coloured', is a tie-dyeing technique for embellishing cloth. It was formerly used by Otomí women in parts of Hidalgo and Querétaro for patterning wrap-around skirts and small *sarapes.* Diamonds, dot formations and flowers were obtained by binding sections of the cloth before immersion in dye. A few elderly women recall the technique and there is hope of a small-scale revival. There is no proof that *plangi* was practised before the Conquest but batik (which relies on wax to repel dye) definitely was, albeit to an unknown degree; today, however, it is found nowhere in Indian Mexico.

Freehand painting is popular in some regions with the makers of woven agave-fibre shoulder-bags. These often display lettering, flowers and fanciful creatures executed with brilliant aniline colours. In rare instances Indians will paint cotton garments: in Ixtayutla, Oaxaca, the Tacuate (who belong to the Mixtec family) daub clothing with a purple colourant using their fingers and thumbs. Colour-stamping is an unusual decorative method which occurs in just a few places. In the Tepehua community of Huehuetla, Hidalgo, *quechquemitl* weavers deliberately imprint the colours of brocaded patterning on to plain white areas. It has been said earlier that commercial dyes often run when clothing is washed; outside observers would probably lament this random streaking of carefully woven or embroidered garments, but results are accepted and sometimes admired by Indian women.

Drawn threadwork

This European technique requires individual threads to be drawn out from the material. The rest are then regrouped, bound to produce a square-meshed ground and reinforced with decorative stitching. Fine nineteenth-century examples from Mexico survive in the textile collection of the Victoria and Albert Museum,

33. Section of a Nahua man's sash from Cuetzalan, Puebla. Both ends have *macramé* fringes worked with needles; wool-embroidered birds and zigzag lines, tassels and sequins provide additional decoration. (Copyright: Marcos Ortiz.)

London (figure 8). Today drawn threadwork is used to embellish the neck and sleeve bands of blouses or the edges of *servilletas*. It also creates occasional areas of decoration on men's shirts and trouser bottoms in the Tacuate village of Santa María Zacatepec, Oaxaca (figure 35).

Lace and crochet

During the long period of colonial rule lace-making was widely taught. Factory lace has now replaced hand-made lace in most parts of Mexico, although Zapotec skirts and head-dresses for festivals still feature wide flounces of genuine lace in Tehuantepec,

Oaxaca. Crochet, which has a shorter history in Mexico, remains popular. It is used by *mestizas* to make *servilletas,* and by Indian women in some regions to create blouse yokes or to edge the neck and arm openings of *huipiles.* Crochet has even been adopted in Nahua villages such as Atla and Xolotla in Puebla to make *quechquemitl:* these are patterned to imitate gauze weaving with animal and plant motifs.

Appliqué
With this technique additional cloth sections are stitched to the main cloth background. Mexican appliqué achieved remarkable delicacy during the nineteenth century. Today shop-bought ribbons are most often used. These may be hemmed into points and sewn round the neck openings of *huipiles,* or laid flat to form decorative bands of colour on blouses, skirts and *huipiles.* Appliquéd ribbons also serve to conceal web joins in some home-woven garments.

Fringing
Before the Conquest various types of fringing were used in Mexico to give garments a decorative finish along their edges. This custom persists, enriched perhaps by similar Spanish traditions. The uncut warps of bags, *servilletas, sarapes,* sashes and *rebozos* are knotted and braided in a variety of ways ranging from the uncomplicated to the highly elaborate (figure 33). Some *rebozo* fringes even depict birds, animals and other figurative designs.

Beadwork
Beadwork achieved great popularity during the nineteenth century, but today rising prices are pushing this form of decoration beyond the reach of many people. In some regions, including the Puebla highlands, small glass beads are sewn down individually on to the yokes and sleeve panels of festival blouses to create shimmering designs. Alternatively, they may be incorporated into areas of crochet. Beads are also knotted into the fringes of *servilletas* in some Tarascan villages in Michoacán. Bags, sashes, hat-bands and jewellery of netted beadwork are made by the Huichol Indians. This last technique is shared, although to a lesser extent, by the Otomí of San Pablito in Puebla.

Other forms of decoration
Love of ornamentation leads many Indian peoples to further embellish garments already replete with woven or embroidered

motifs. Colourful cascades of ribbons are attached to the back of some Trique *huipiles*; pompoms adorn the corners of Huichol and Cora shoulder-bags; sequins are sewn haphazardly on to Nahua skirts in Acatlán, Guerrero, or on to fiesta *huipiles* in the Chinantec village of San Lucas Ojitlán, Oaxaca; non-functional buttons, tassels and silvery butterfly chrysalises decorate men's shirt fronts in Tacuate villages in Oaxaca.

Pleating is an important skill in parts of Michoacán, where Tarascan women favour heavy skirts of red or blue-black wool. Cloth is folded when damp and left under a heavy weight for several days. When worn, skirts lie flat at the front but display thick European-style pleats behind. Tailored embellishments such as ruffles and tucks are generally confined to non-indigenous garments such as blouses, shirts and gathered skirts on waistbands. There has been a tendency in recent years, however, for Chinantec and Mazatec women in certain Oaxacan villages to add 'sleeves' of ribbons and factory lace to their *huipiles*.

34. Tapestry-patterned *sarape* with *kelim*-style neck opening, woven from undyed wool on a treadle loom in Coatepec Harinas, Mexico State. The warp yarns form a fringe at both ends (not shown). 38½ by 67½ inches (97.8 by 171.5 cm). (Copyright: David Lavender.)

5
Contemporary Indian costume

Male dress

Since the Spanish Conquest male native dress has undergone more changes than female dress. Indian men habitually travel further from their communities than women and their clothing is often shop-bought and indistinguishable from that of non-Indians. Over the last few decades several fine costumes have died out, but a few groups still adhere to more traditional styles of dress. In Chiapas, for example, many Lacandón men still wear *huipil*-like tunics of cotton cloth, while the Tarahumara of Chihuahua frequently use cotton loincloths during hot weather with just a woollen sash for support.

European garments such as shirts and trousers have been interpreted in a variety of ways throughout Indian Mexico. Generally they are loose-fitting and constructed without the aid of zips or buttons. Handsome and distinctive examples are still woven on backstrap looms in Tzotzil and Tzeltal villages in the Chiapas highlands, as well as in parts of Oaxaca. More commonly, however, they are made from white factory-made cotton cloth. Huichol men, who take enormous pride in their clothing, wear richly embroidered shirts and trousers of calico with a profusion of woven sashes and bags of wool or acrylic.

Shoulder-bags are popular not just with the Huichol. To make up for the lack of pockets in Indian dress, they are carried by men from all regions. Hats constitute another essential costume element. Even with shop- or market-bought hats it is usually possible to tell at a glance where the wearer is from, since most states have evolved a particular design. The greatest diversity is to be found with home-made hats, however. These include increasingly rare examples of black felt from Oaxaca and a wide range of palm styles variously decorated with woven bands, netted beadwork, feathers or tassels. Leather sandals, often with car-tyre soles, may be bought or made at home.

In country regions the *sarape* is often worn during cold weather by Indians and non-Indians alike. Despite rising sales of acrylic factory-made styles, treadle-loom workshops exist in numerous centres throughout Mexico to meet the continuing demand for durable wool-woven *sarapes*. More rarely these or similar top garments may be woven on backstrap looms. In Chiapas, for example, Tzotzil weavers from San Juan Chamula weave thick and virtually

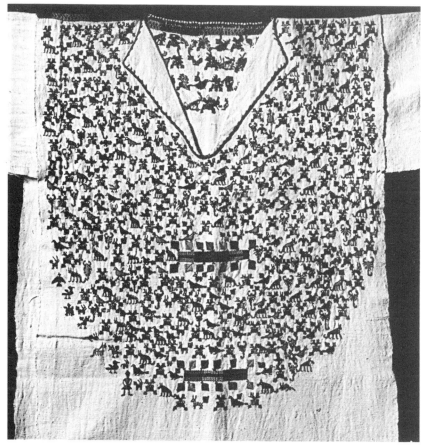

35. Tacuate (Mixtec) man's shirt from Santa María Zacatepec, Oaxaca. Woven from hand-spun cotton on a backstrap loom, it features drawn threadwork and embroidery. (Copyright: Museum of Mankind.)

rainproof garments from white or black wool. Their felt-like texture is achieved by washing, beating and shrinking the cloth. Rain-capes, made by knotting palm-leaf strips into superimposed layers, are still used in parts of Mexico, despite the spread of plastic sheeting.

Female dress

In many parts of Indian Mexico women's costume has changed surprisingly little since the Conquest. Wrap-around skirts are assembled and worn in a number of ways. Cloth rectangles, consisting of a single web or of two or more webs joined horizontally, are wrapped about the limbs in the manner of a sarong or sewn to form a tube and wrapped to create a series of often voluminous folds and pleats. Waist-sashes are used in most communities to keep skirts in place; dimensions vary considerably, but the largest sashes are probably those woven in the Zapotec village of Santo Tomás Mazaltepec, Oaxaca. These have an average width of 17 inches (32 cm) and a length of 130 inches (330 cm). In parts of Oaxaca and Puebla woven cloth sashes are used over tubular extensions of plaited palm.

Before the Conquest *huipiles* and *quechquemitl* often existed simultaneously and were on occasion worn together. Today the two garments virtually never coincide. The *huipil* is currently confined to areas of Morelos, Michoacán, Guerrero, Oaxaca, Chiapas

36. Tarahumara man's sash of undyed wool, woven with warp patterning on a rigid loom of logs. 3¾ by 80 inches (9.5 by 203.2 cm) including the fringe. (Copyright: David Lavender.)

37. *Huipil* constructions. One web: (A) Venustiano Carranza, Chiapas; (B) Tuxpan, Jalisco. Two webs: (C) Yalalag, Oaxaca. Three webs: (D) San Andrés Larrainzar, Chiapas. Four webs: (E) Santiago Temoaya, Mexico State.

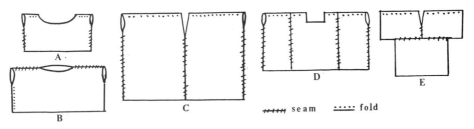

and the Yucatán Peninsula; it also occurs in isolated Nahua villages in Jalisco, Veracruz and south-east Puebla, and among the Otomí of Santiago Temoaya in Mexico State. Patterning, construction methods, proportions and styles of wearing vary widely. Some *huipiles* are made from one web or four webs, although two and especially three webs are more commonly used. Short garments may be tucked inside the skirt, but longer ones hang freely, occasionally concealing the skirt altogether. Sides are sometimes left virtually unsewn. In several villages gala *huipiles* differ from everyday styles. The pre-Hispanic custom of incorporating feathers into cloth seems to have died out everywhere in Mexico except Zinacantán, Chiapas. Here Tzotzil women embellish wedding *huipiles* with weft threads which have been interspun with downy white chicken feathers.

The *quechquemitl* is worn today by the Huichol, the Huastec, the Mazahua, the Tepehua, the Totonac, the Otomí and the Nahua, who together employ an astonishing variety of weaving, embroidery and other decorative techniques. Two basic construction methods persist (figure 38). The second type has the widest distribution and, as shown in the diagram, points fall either to the front and back, or to the sides.

38. Contemporary *quechquemitl* constructions.

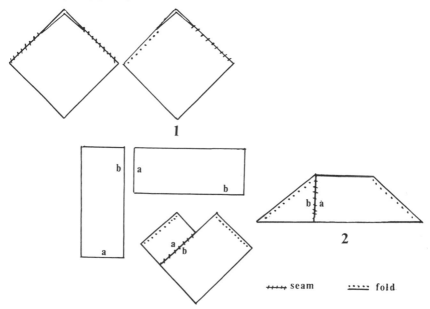

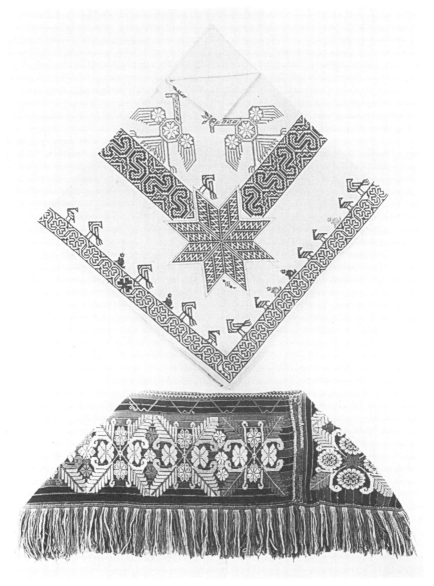

39. *Quechquemitl.* (Top) Construction 1, made from factory cloth and embroidered with cross and long-armed cross stitches. Huichol; Jalisco. 23½ inches (59.7 cm) square. (Bottom) Construction 2, woven on a backstrap loom and embroidered in cross stitch, with an added fringe. Strips measure 28 by 10½ inches (71.1 by 26.7 cm) and have needle-formed joins. Mazahua; Santa Ana Eyenzú, Mexico. (Copyright: David Lavender.)

40. Ceremonial brocade-patterned *huipil*, woven on a backstrap loom from cotton and naturally dyed wool in Magdalenas, Chiapas. Designs and colours convey elements of Tzotzil cosmology. 33 by 27½ inches (83.8 by 69.8 cm). (Copyright: David Lavender.)

Quechquemitl are smaller than they once were. This may be because women are unwilling to cover the ever-increasing decoration on blouses. Introduced into *quechquemitl* areas after the Conquest for reasons of modesty, the blouse is now gaining popularity in *huipil* regions and has altogether replaced this ancient garment in some villages. In others *huipiles* may be given sleeve-like trimmings to emulate the blouse. Indian ingenuity has resulted in a wide range of embellishment for blouses. In the Puebla highlands they are distinguished by angularity of shape: box-cut and totally unfitted, they are fashioned from straight panels of factory cloth. Other European garments to have found favour in Indian Mexico include gathered skirts on waistbands and aprons.

Indian women use a wide range of coverings and head-dresses according to region. In some villages woven cloths serve as capes but are also used to carry loads and babies. In strong sunlight heads may be covered with folded cloths, a second *quechquemitl* or even a palm hat, but the *rebozo*, or rectangular shawl, remains the most popular all-purpose protective garment, doubling when necessary as a carrying cloth. Elaborate methods of styling hair exist in a few areas; these rely on thick woollen cords or woven ribbons. Few communities possess standardised footwear for women and many still go barefoot, while others have adopted sandals or factory-made shoes. Jewellery is enjoyed throughout Indian Mexico and is often worn in profusion.

Conclusion

Indian costume has never been static. After the Conquest it absorbed many European features and more recently garments in numerous communities have become increasingly decorated as factory threads and trimmings became more readily available. But there has been a decline in standards in the later twentieth century. Materials such as wool are expensive and in short supply. Commercial cloth has replaced home-woven cloth in many areas where women continue to make traditional garments. In Cuetzalan in Puebla, for example, many Nahua women now use factory lace to simulate gauze-weaving. Such trends often mark a period of transition, leading ultimately to the adoption of Western clothing.

Costume is bound up with a range of social issues and is closely linked with the self-image of Indian peoples. For the Huichol, who continue to take great pride in their own culture, costume has retained much of the religious symbolism and ceremonial importance described at the beginning of the twentieth century by Carl Lumholtz (figure 41); when the Huichol leave the remote *sierra* where they live to visit Guadalajara or Mexico City, they wear their often magnificent costumes with confidence. Most other Indians have closer ties with the non-Indian world, however. Many have become sensitive to the attitudes of local people, who often equate the wearing of traditional clothing with backwardness. In order to avoid embarrassment Indians will sometimes cover village garments with shop-bought ones when visiting large markets or adopt *mestizo* clothing altogether when going into towns or cities. Eventual assimilation into the national culture has, in many cases, entailed the loss of ancient cultural traits such as language and costume. It would be sad if Indian costume, together with textile skills that have endured for countless centuries, should disappear altogether from Mexico.

6
Glossary

Agave: genus of succulent plants with stiff leaves from the New World. Long and durable fibres are obtained from several species.

Appliqué: technique whereby shaped sections of cloth are stitched to a cloth background.

Batik: method for resist-dyeing cloth. Designs are created by applying a waxy substance to selected areas, rendering them impervious to dye.

Brocade weaving: technique whereby supplementary threads are used to create superstructural patterning in cloth while it is on the loom.

Coyuche: natural brown cotton *(Gossypium mexicanum*; from the Náhuatl *coyoichcatl)*.

Double weaving: when two layers of warp threads are periodically interchanged, double cloth is created. Patterning is identical on both sides of the cloth, but the positions of ground and motifs are reversed.

Drawn threadwork: technique whereby individual threads are drawn out from cloth.

Gauze weaving: selected warp threads are crossed and secured by the weft to create cloth with an open, lace-like texture.

Huipil: woman's sleeveless tunic (from the Náhuatl *huipilli)*.

Ikat: method for tie-dyeing yarn.

Mestizo: Mexican of mixed European and Indian descent.

Netting: technique which relies on the looping or knotting of a single element.

Plain weaving: basic construction where each weft thread passes over and under one warp thread.

Plangi: method for patterning cloth by tie-dyeing.

Quechquemitl: woman's closed shoulder-cape (Náhuatl term).

Rebozo: woman's rectangular shawl.

Sarape: blanket, often with an opening for the head.

Servilleta: cloth, often used for ceremonial purposes or to cover food.

Tapestry weaving: technique for creating designs in cloth using weft threads which move across selected areas and not from selvage to selvage.

Twill weaving: diagonal lines are formed in the cloth as warp threads are regularly positioned to the left or right of successive weft threads.

41. Huichol man from San Andrés Cohamiata, Jalisco, painting his face for a festival. He wears a necklace and bracelet of netted beadwork, woven sashes and a richly embroidered shirt and shoulder-bag. (Copyright: Marcos Ortiz.)

Twining: technique whereby two or more weft threads are twisted around each other to enclose one or more warp threads.

Warp patterning: warp threads periodically cross varying numbers of weft threads to form raised designs in the cloth.

Weft loop weaving: supplementary weft threads are looped with a pick to form raised superstructural patterning.

7
Museums

The following museums have Mexican textiles; these are not always on public display but may sometimes be seen by appointment. Intending visitors are advised to find out the opening times before making a special journey.

United Kingdom

Museum of Mankind (the Ethnography Department of the British Museum), 6 Burlington Gardens, London W1X 2EX. Telephone: 01-437 2224.

Pitt Rivers Museum, South Parks Road, Oxford OX1 3PP. Telephone: 0865 270927.

Victoria and Albert Museum, Cromwell Road, South Kensington, London SW7 2RL. Telephone: 01-938 8500.
Whitworth Art Gallery, University of Manchester, Oxford Road, Manchester M15 6ER. Telephone: 061-273 4865.

France
Musée de l'Homme, Palais de Chaillot, Place du Trocadéro, 75016 Paris.

Germany West
Museum für Völkerkunde, Arnimalee 23-27, 1000 Berlin 33.
Staatliches Museum für Völkerkunde, Schaumainkai 29, 6000 Frankfurt 70.

Mexico
Museo de la Indumentaria Mexicana 'Luis Marquez', José Ma. Izazaga 80, Col. Centro, Mexico City.
Museo Nacional de Antropología, Paseo de la Reforma (Bosque de Chapultepec), Mexico City.
Museo Nacional de Artes e Industrias Populares del INI, Avenida Juárez 44, Mexico City.
Museo Regional de Oaxaca, Ex Convento de Santo Domingo, Oaxaca City.

Netherlands
Rijksmuseum voor Volkenkunde, Steenstraat 1, 2300 AE Leiden, Zuid Holland.

Spain
Museu Etnològic, Paseo de Santa Madrona, Parque de Montjuïc, 08004 Barcelona.

Sweden
Göteborgs Etnografiska Museet, Norra Hamngatan 12, 41114 Gothenburg.

United States of America
American Museum of Natural History, 79th Street and Central Park West, New York, NY 10024.
Arizona State Museum, University of Arizona, Tucson, Arizona 85721.
Brooklyn Museum, 188 Eastern Parkway, Brooklyn, New York, NY 11238.

Heard Museum, 22 East Monte Vista Road, Phoenix, Arizona 85004.
Mexican Museum, Fort Mason, Building D, Laguna and Marina Boulevard, San Francisco, California 94123.
Museum of International Folk Art, PO Box 2087, Santa Fe, New Mexico 87504.
San Diego Museum of Man, 1350 El Prado, Balboa Park, San Diego, California 92101.
Smithsonian Institution, 1000 Jefferson Drive SW, Washington DC 20560.
Textile Museum, 2320 South Street NW, Washington DC 20008.

8
Further reading

Broudy, Eric. *The Book of Looms: A History of the Handloom from Ancient Times to the Present*. Studio Vista, London, 1979.
Burnham, Dorothy K. *Warp and Weft: a Textile Terminology*. Royal Ontario Museum, Toronto, 1980.
Clabburn, Pamela. *The Needleworker's Dictionary*. Macmillan, London, 1976.
Cordry, Donald B. and Dorothy M. *Mexican Indian Costumes*. University of Texas Press, Austin, 1968.
Jeter, James, and Juelke, Paula Marie. *The Saltillo Sarape*. Exhibition Catalogue of the Museum of Art, Santa Barbara, 1978.
Johnson, Irmgard Weitlaner. *Design Motifs on Mexican Indian Textiles* (two volumes). Akademische Druck-und-Verlagsanstalt, Graz, 1976.
Larsen, Jack L., *et al. The Dyer's Art: Ikat, Batik and Plangi*. Nostrand Reinhold, New York, 1976.
Morris, Walter F., Junior. *A Millennium of Weaving in Chiapas*. Private printing by the author for distribution by Sna Jolobil, the Chiapas Maya Weavers' Association, Mexico, 1984.
Sayer, Chloë. *Mexican Costume*. British Museum Publications, London, 1985.
Start, Laura E. *The McDougall Collection of Indian Textiles from Guatemala and Mexico*. Pitt Rivers Museum, Oxford, 1980.
Sutton, Ann, *et al. The Craft of the Weaver*. BBC Books, London, 1982.
Taber, Barbara, and Anderson, Marilyn. *Backstrap Weaving*. Watson-Guptill Publications, New York, 1975.

Index

Page numbers in italic refer to illustrations